WOODWORK THEORY
BOOK ONE

WOODWORK THEORY

BOOK ONE

P. F. LYE
Thomas More Secondary School
Purley, Surrey

HARRAP   LONDON

First published in Great Britain 1967
by GEORGE G. HARRAP & CO. LTD
182-184 High Holborn, London WC1V 7AX

Metric Edition 1971

Reprinted: 1972; 1973; 1975; 1976 *(twice)*; 1977;
       1978

© *P. F. Lye* 1967, 1971

ISBN 0 245 50644 6

Printed in Great Britain by
Biddles Ltd, Guildford, Surrey

CONTENTS

To the Teacher

These books are intended to supplement the teaching given in the workshop, either in conjunction with supervised work in school or for homework.

The Sections do not have to be used in the order in which they are presented here but can easily be integrated into your own teaching scheme.

To the Student

Before answering the questions, carefully read the Section concerned and examine the drawing if one is provided. You should then find the questions quite easy to answer.

Answer in complete sentences and make your writing clear and neat.

Your drawings should be as large as possible but certainly not smaller than the ones in the book. Sketch your drawings very lightly to begin with and when you have the outline well spaced on the paper it can be filled in firmly and detail added.

You should be able to answer every question correctly.

Look after your book carefully and take a pride in your work.

THE BENCH

A good workbench is essential for anyone who wishes to do woodwork properly. Unfortunately, the workbench is often the most neglected part of the woodwork equipment. The benches provided for school woodwork are good solid benches, made of red beech. They should be looked after by all students with care.

Each side of the bench is fitted with a vice for holding wood. This is often of the quick release type. The jaws are lined with wood. The inside of these jaws should not be damaged by gripping metal objects. The wooden parts of the vice must not be planed, sawn or damaged in any way. A bench hook (see Section 33 No. 1) is held in the vice for sawing with the tenon saw.

An adjustable bench stop is provided for holding wood that is being planed on top of the bench. These stops are made for right handed people. However, many teachers put left-handed bench stops on some benches. The bench stop should always be lower than the wood being planed or it will be damaged. A little linseed oil helps it to move freely for adjustment.

The central part of the bench top is lower, this is called the well. Tools that are in use should be laid out in the well of the bench and not spread untidily all over the top of the bench. Tools not in use should be kept in the tool rack.

The good surface of the bench should be the concern of every-one who uses it. For example when sawing in the vice, a piece of waste wood should be placed on the bench under the saw. This will protect the bench from possible damage. Chiselling should not be done directly on to the bench top. A piece of waste wood should be underneath the work to protect the bench.

When using paint, stain, or polish, the surface of the bench must be covered with a board or paper. When drilling or using nails, care must be taken that holes are not made in the bench.

At the end of each work period, the bench should be swept down. The next person to use the bench should find it clean and with the tools in the correct place.

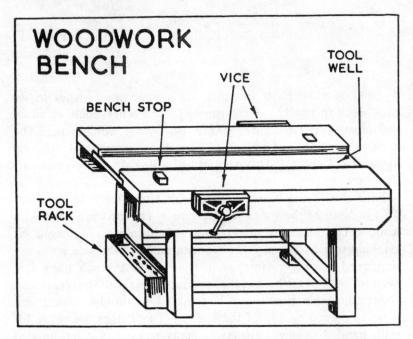

WOODWORK BENCH

VICE

TOOL WELL

BENCH STOP

TOOL RACK

Questions

1. Reproduce the drawing of a woodwork bench shown above.
2. For what purpose would you use (*a*) the bench stop (*b*) the vice?
3. State how you would protect the bench from possible damage (*a*) when sawing in the vice (*b*) when painting on the bench (*c*) when chiselling on the bench.
4. Complete the following sentence correctly, using (*a*) or (*b*) or (*c*): When planing on top of the bench, the bench stop should be adjusted to come (*a*) level with the top of the wood, (*b*) slightly below the top of the wood, (*c*) above the top of the wood.
5. What type of wood is used to make school woodwork benches ?

THE RULE

The rule is used for measuring. Measurement is often necess-ary in woodwork, and it is important that all measurement is very accurately performed. The student must therefore learn to use his rule with ease and precision.

Measurements on the rule are taken from the end. In this respect the rule used by woodworkers is not the same as the ruler in general use in the classroom.

The majority of rules provided for school workshops are of the 300 mm rustless steel type. Many carpenters prefer a wooden

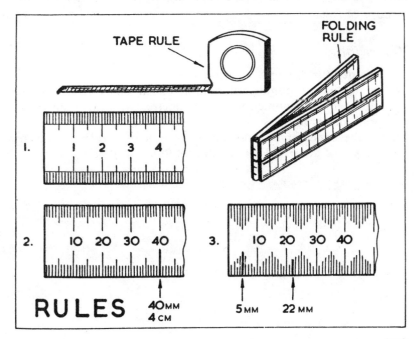

RULES

rule but as these break quite easily they are not very suitable for school use. In recent years white nylon rules have become very popular and they are much tougher than the wooden ones. For long measurement up to 2 or 3 metres a steel tape rule is very useful. A combined metre rule and straight edge (see Section 33 No. 8) is also a useful piece of equipment.

Readings on the rule are generally taken in millimetres but for very long measurements the metre unit is sometimes used. The centimetre unit is seldom used. Readings on the metric rule are very simple as there are ten millimetres in one centimetre and one hundred centimetres in one metre. There will thus be one thousand millimetres in one metre. The abbreviation for millimetre is mm, for centimetre cm and for metre m.

Several main types of rule divisions are shown on page 11. No. 1 shows a rule divided into centimetres and millimetres. No. 2 shows a rule divided into millimetres. The millimetre is a very small unit and it is quite easy to make an error in reading. The rule shown at No. 3 has divisions of different length and this makes it easier to read the number of millimetres required. In any case all millimetre rules are divided by a larger division into groups of five.

Questions

1 Name four different types of rule.
2 State (a) the number of millimetres in one metre. (b) the number of centimetres in one metre. (c) the number of millimetres in one centimetre.
3. Make an enlarged drawing of 30 mm of a rule. Show by means of an arrow (a) 16 mm, (b) 9 mm, (c) 2 cm.

THE PENCIL AND MARKING KNIFE

Two of the chief tools used for marking are the pencil and the marking knife. The pencil is in general use for much of the marking required. The knife is used for very accurate marking of joints which must fit tightly.

Pencils must be kept sharp. The degree of hardness of the pencil lead is stamped on one end of the pencil. An HB pencil is quite satisfactory, but many craftsmen prefer a 2H. This is harder and therefore gives a thinner line.

The marking knife consists of a short blade held in a wooden handle. Although it is used for marking joints, it must be used with care. Remember that a marking knife line will not rub off even with glasspaper. The appearance would be spoilt by marking knife lines showing on your finished work. Only those

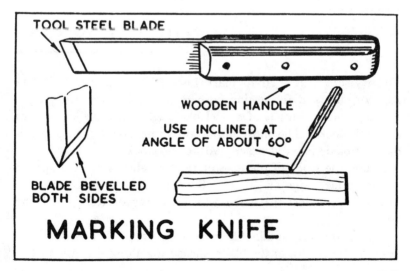

TOOL STEEL BLADE

WOODEN HANDLE

USE INCLINED AT
ANGLE OF ABOUT 60°

BLADE BEVELLED
BOTH SIDES

MARKING KNIFE

lines on which a cut is going to be made should be marked with a knife.

When using a pencil or marking knife to mark with the try-square (see Section 4), the knife or pencil should be inclined at an angle of about 60° (see drawing). In this way the line marked will be accurately aligned with the edge of the square.

The pencil is used to mark the face side and face edge (see Section 7) to mark waste wood with a cross and to number joints. All unnecessary pencil marks should be avoided. Necessary marking should be neat. Remember these marks will probably have to be cleaned off when the work is finished.

Questions

1. Reproduce the drawing of a marking knife.
2. Name three types of marking for which you would use a pencil and give a reason why you would not use a marking knife for these.
3. Complete the following sentence correctly using (a) or (b): The marking knife is used (a) when marking lines on which an accurate cut is to be made, (b) when the pencil is not clear enough.

SECTION 4

THE TRY SQUARE

The try-square is used to mark lines at right angles to a true edge or side and for testing corners to see if these are square. The try-square consists of a steel blade set in either a wooden or a metal stock. The most important thing about the square is that the blade is set at exactly 90° to the stock.

In use, the stock of the try-square must always be held against a true or face edge or side (see Section 7). The stock must be held firmly against the wood while marking or testing is being done.

Try-squares are obtainable in various sizes. The size is indicated by the length of the blade, measuring along the inside edge.

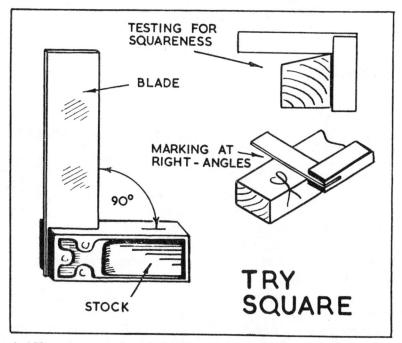

TESTING FOR SQUARENESS

BLADE

MARKING AT RIGHT-ANGLES

90°

STOCK

TRY SQUARE

A 150 mm square is suitable for most bench work. Most workshops have also a 300 mm square for marking across wide boards.

Care must be taken when using the square. It should not be dropped or damaged in any way or the blade may become out of 'true'. The truth of the square may be tested by marking a line at right angles to a very accurate face edge. The square is then turned over and another line marked in the same place. If the square is true the two lines will be identical. If the square is not true, any inaccuracy will be doubled and would show by the two lines not being parallel.

Questions

1. Name two purposes for which a try-square is used.
2. Reproduce the drawing of a try-square given above.
3. How is the size of a try-square indicated ? Name two useful sizes of try-square.
4. Complete the following sentence correctly using (*a*) or (*b*): In use the square is always held (*a*) with the stock against the true edge or side. (*b*) with the blade against the true edge or side.

SECTION 5

THE TENON SAW

The tenon saw is used for light bench work, for cutting wood of small section to length and for cutting joints. It is particularly well suited for cutting tenons (see Sections 25, 28) hence its name.

The tenon saw has a stiffening rib along the length of the blade. This prevents the blade bending, it is therefore easier to make a straight cut. The stiffening rib is made either of brass or steel. The blade is made of high quality cast steel, hardened and tempered.

Tenon saws are obtainable in several different lengths. The shortest saws are 200 mm long, the longest are 400 mm. Tenon saws provided for school use are usually 300 mm long.

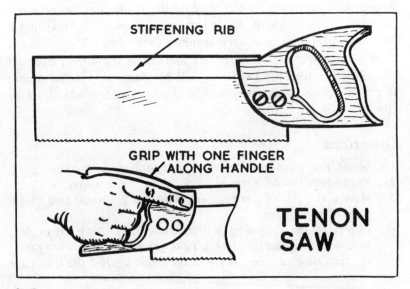

STIFFENING RIB

GRIP WITH ONE FINGER ALONG HANDLE

TENON SAW

The size of the teeth on the tenon saw is important. The size of the teeth is indicated by the number of teeth per inch (T.P.I.). A fine toothed saw may have as many as 16 T.P.I. 12 or 14 T.P.I. is more usual. (See Section 33 No. 10).

The tenon saw must be treated with great care. The small teeth are easily damaged. Although the saw may be re-sharpened and set, this is not easily done. A damaged saw will not cut properly. The saw should not be left on the bench where it may strike metal tools. It is better to put it in the tool rack when not in use.

When using the saw the handle should be gripped firmly with the first finger along the length of the saw (see drawing) This gives increased control over the saw. When starting a saw cut it will be found helpful to draw the saw back two or three times first to mark the position of the cut. The cut should, of course, be made on the waste wood side of the line.

Questions

1. Name two purposes for which a tenon saw would be used.
2. Reproduce the drawing of a tenon saw given opposite.
3. State: (a) The usual length of tenon saw provided for school use. (b) The usual number of teeth per inch for a tenon saw.
4. Complete the following passage correctly using (a) or (b): The tenon saw has a stiffening rib along the back. The purpose of this is (a) to stop the saw cutting too deep, (b) to prevent the blade bending when in use.

SECTION 6

THE JACK PLANE

The jack plane may be used for quite a variety of different planing jobs. It may be used for smoothing the surface of rough sawn wood, for planing an uneven surface straight and true, and for cutting away waste wood down to a finishing line.

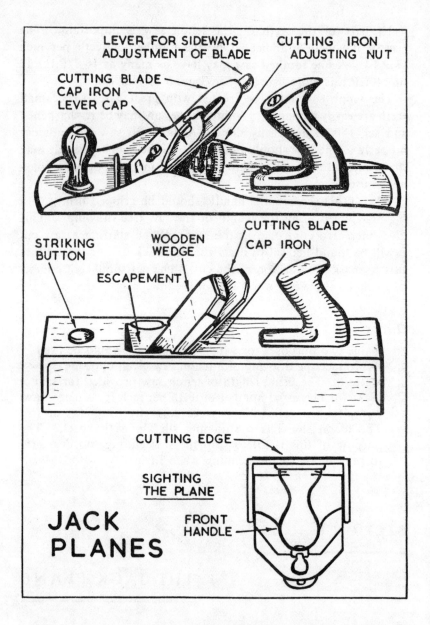

LEVER FOR SIDEWAYS
ADJUSTMENT OF BLADE

CUTTING IRON
ADJUSTING NUT

CUTTING BLADE
CAP IRON
LEVER CAP

STRIKING
BUTTON

WOODEN
WEDGE

CUTTING BLADE
CAP IRON

ESCAPEMENT

CUTTING EDGE

SIGHTING
THE PLANE

JACK
PLANES

FRONT
HANDLE

Jack planes are of two main types: wooden jack planes and steel jack planes. The wooden jack plane is made of red beech and is frequently used in school workshops. It is a strong and efficient tool when correctly adjusted, However. some skill is required to adjust it correctly. This does not apply to the steel jack plane which is quickly and easily adjusted to suit all planing needs.

The blade and cap iron (see Section 8) of a wooden jack plane are held in position by a wooden wedge. In order to adjust the cutting iron, this wedge must be loosened. The wedge is loosened by hitting the striking button (see drawing) with a mallet. The plane is held in the palm of the hand, the thumb being placed in the escapement to hold the cutting iron. When the cutting iron is set so that the cutting edge is just within the mouth of the plane the wedge is tapped down lightly to hold it. The plane is now turned upside-down and 'sighted' along the sole. The cutting edge should not be visible. The cutting iron is now gently tapped down with a hammer until the cutting edge is just visible as a thin black line. The wedge is given another tap to make sure that the cutting iron is set firmly and the plane is then tested. If a heavier cut is required, the cutting iron must be tapped down a little further with a hammer. If it is set too coarse, the whole process must be repeated.

By comparison, adjustment of the steel jack plane is extremely easy. An adjusting nut is situated behind the blade. When rotated this nut moves a lever which is fitted into the cap iron. If the nut is rotated clockwise the blade is moved down to make a coarser cut. If the nut is rotated anti-clockwise the blade is raised to make a finer cut. A lever which moves sideways is also situated behind the blade. This is used to move the cutting edge of the blade down on one side or the other. Complete control over the adjustment of the blade is therefore made easy.

Sometimes the mouth of the plane may become clogged with shavings. This is generally caused by having the cutting iron set to take too large a shaving, which then becomes jammed in the mouth of the plane. It is sometimes caused by an incorrectly set or faulty cap iron (see Section 8). Some woods tend to clog the plane more than others. If the mouth becomes clogged with shavings, the cutting iron must be removed and the mouth cleared. The mouth should never be cleared from the outside as this would damage the cutting edge of the blade.

Questions

1. Name two types of jack plane.

2. Reproduce the drawing of one of the jack planes shown on page 18.
3. Two jack planes, (a) a wooden jack plane, and (b) a steel jack plane, are set too coarse. Describe how you would re-set each to make a finer cut.
4. Name two planing operations for which a jack plane would be used.

SECTION 7

USING THE JACK PLANE

The jack plane cuts away the wood in the form of small shavings. Clearly care must be taken to remove shavings only where needed, otherwise the wood will not be finished to the required size. It is much easier to plane wood accurately if a few simple rules are followed.

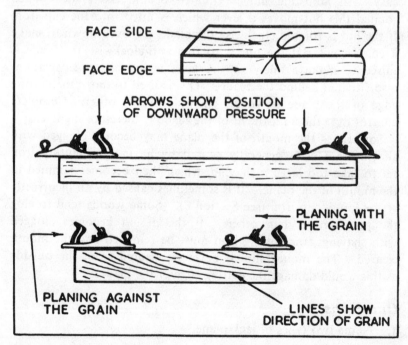

Let us imagine that we have a piece of sawn softwood 300 mm long, 50 mm wide and 25 mm thick. We require to plane this to finish to 46 mm × 21 mm.

The first thing we must do is to sight the plane (see Section 6) to make sure the blade is correctly adjusted. It must not be set too coarse. The wider surface of the wood, called the side, is generally planed first, not the edge. The wood is placed flat on the bench, the end of the wood being set against the bench stop (see Section 1). We have first to prepare a true side which will be called the 'face side'. Face marks are shown on the sketch opposite.

Assuming that the operator is right handed, his right side should be against the bench. The plane is operated from behind in order to give plenty of punch. At the start of the cut, the main pressure should be on the forward part of the plane. During the latter part of the cut the main pressure should be at the back of the plane (see sketch opposite). Each stroke should, if possible, be taken through the full length of the piece of wood.

When planed, the surface must be tested for accuracy. This is done by placing the steel rule or straight edge on the wood. The two are then 'sighted' together to see whether the surface of the wood is true with the straight edge. When this surface is true it may be marked with a face side mark.

An adjacent edge must now be prepared in the same way to provide a face edge. This must not only be straight but it must also be square with the face side.

All marking or testing is done from the face side or face edge. These must, therefore, be accurate. It is not easy to prepare a face side and face edge true, but the student should not be satisfied with inaccurately prepared surfaces.

With surfaces accurately prepared the wood may now be marked to width. This is done with a marking gauge (see Section 9). The gauge must be used with the stock against the face edge. Care must be taken not to plane beyond the gauge line.

The wood is now marked to thickness, again using the gauge and the wood is then planed to the gauge line.

In this way all four sides of the wood are planed and the wood is true and finished to the correct size. If the wood is not accurately prepared this will be very obvious in any joints that are made with it later.

It frequently happens that wood planes better in one direction than the other. This is due to the direction of the grain. If a piece of wood tends to tear up, turn it round and try the other way.

The planing of end grain (see Section 12) is rather more difficult. It should not be attempted at this stage without special instruction.

Great care should be taken of the cutting edge of the plane. Place the plane down on the bench sideways or over the well of the bench in order not to damage the cutting edge.

Questions

1. Describe, stage by stage, how you would plane a face side and face edge on a piece of softwood 300 × 75 × 25 mm.
2. Show by means of a sketch the downward pressure on the plane (a) at the start of a stroke, (b) at the end of a stroke.
3. Why do you 'sight' the plane before using it?
4. Make a sketch to show the traditional face marks.
5. Describe how you would test the face side of a piece of wood for flatness.

SECTION 8

THE PLANE CUTTING IRONS

The cutting iron fitted to the jack plane, try-plane, and smoothing plane, consists of two parts. The blade has the cutting edge at one end. This cuts the wood. The cap iron is attached to the blade. The main function of the cap iron is to break up the shavings and thus prevent the wood surface from tearing. It also guides the shavings through the plane and helps to prevent vibration of the blade.

Let us consider first the blade. The thin blade that is provided with steel planes is made of cast steel (see Section 33 No. 4). The heavier blade provided with wooden planes has a piece of cast steel welded on to a mild steel body, the cast steel forming the cutting edge. The reason for this is two-fold. A thick cast steel blade would not be so easy to grind, and cast steel when repeatedly struck with a hammer would fracture.

The cutting edge of the blade is sharpened with two sharpening angles. Firstly the cutting edge is ground on a grindstone to an angle of about 25°. Secondly the cutting edge is sharpened on an oilstone to an angle of about 30° (see drawing). The blade requires sharpening frequently. It does not need grinding very often. It will be seen from the drawing, that by providing two angles, the whole thickness of the blade does not have to be sharpened on the oilstone.

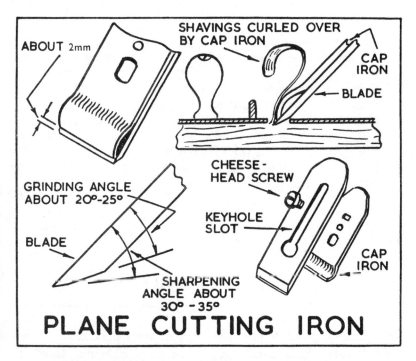

ABOUT 2mm

SHAVINGS CURLED OVER BY CAP IRON

CAP IRON

BLADE

GRINDING ANGLE ABOUT 20°-25°

CHEESE-HEAD SCREW

KEYHOLE SLOT

BLADE

SHARPENING ANGLE ABOUT 30° - 35°

CAP IRON

PLANE CUTTING IRON

Many craftsmen like to have the cutting edge very slightly rounded to form a convex cutting edge. It is also quite common practice to round off the corners so that these do not leave marks on the wood being planed.

The cutting iron has a 'keyhole slot' down the centre. A cheese head screw through this slot attaches the cap iron to the blade. The cap iron is made of mild steel. The lower edge is curved over in such a way that when tightened it will press down near the edge of the cutting iron. The cap iron must fit well on the blade or shavings will get between and clog the mouth of the plane.

On jack planes the edge of the cap iron is set about 2 mm back from the cutting edge of the blade. On smoothing planes and try-planes the cap iron is set closer to the cutting edge. This helps to give a smoother finish to the wood being planed but it limits the degree of coarseness to which the plane may be set. When the cutting iron is placed in the plane, the cap iron should be uppermost and to the front.

Questions

1. Name the two parts of a jack plane cutting iron.
2. Reproduce the drawing of a jack plane blade and cap iron.
3. Show by means of a sketch the sharpening and grinding angles on a jack plane blade.
4. Complete the following sentence correctly, using (a) or (b): The cutting iron should be placed in the plane (a) with the cap iron uppermost, (b) with the blade uppermost.
5. Show by means of a sketch how the cap iron curves and breaks the shavings.

SECTION 9

THE MARKING GAUGE

The marking gauge is used for marking lines parallel to a true edge or side. This is necessary when wood is being planed to width and thickness. It is also frequently necessary when marking out joints.

The marking gauge is generally used along the grain of the wood. (see Section 12). It may be used quite well on end grain, but it tends to tear and scratch when used across the grain.

The marking gauge consists of four parts. The stock has a hole through the centre the stem is a sliding fit in this. The fit must be tight or the stem will wobble in use. Sometimes the stock contains brass bearing strips to reduce wear. The stem has a cast steel spur inserted near one end. This marks the wood and the point should not project more than 4 mm through the stem. The gauge is usually made of red beech with the exception of the thumbscrew which is made of boxwood or plastic.

To set the gauge first release the thumbscrew, then set the gauge placing the end of the rule against the stock (see drawing). It is usual to hold the stock and to tap the stem on the bench to move it to the required setting. When set correctly the thumbscrew is tightened and the setting checked before use.

The gauge is not a very easy tool for the beginner to use. But as it is such a useful tool, its correct use should be mastered. There are three points to remember when using the gauge. The stock must be pressed firmly against the face edge. The gauge should be pushed in a direction away from the operator. The spur should be allowed to trail, a slight pressure being applied. (The drawing below will illustrate this.) This spur should not be upright or it will tend to dig in. Several strokes may be needed to produce a clear line. It will sometimes be found helpful to

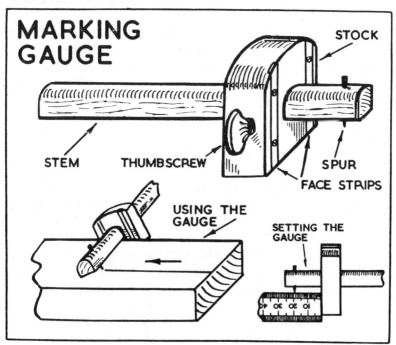

MARKING GAUGE

STOCK

STEM   THUMBSCREW   SPUR

FACE STRIPS

USING THE GAUGE

SETTING THE GAUGE

hold the wood in the bench vice while it is being marked. This will leave both hands free to hold the gauge.

Questions

1. What material is used to make (a) the gauge, (b) the spur of the gauge, and (c) the thumbscrew of the gauge ?
2. Reproduce the drawing of a marking gauge.
3. Make a sketch to show the method of using a marking gauge.
4. Make a sketch to show how the gauge is set from the end of the rule.
5. Complete the following sentence correctly, using (a) or (b): The marking gauge is used for marking lines, (a) parallel to a true edge or side, (b) at right angles to a true edge or side.

SECTION 10

THE CROSS HALVING JOINT

The cross halving joint is used when two pieces of wood have to be joined to form a cross. This is sometimes necessary. For example the diagonal under-rails of tables are joined in this way. The joint may also be used to join the parts of a framework such as that of a shed, or to join the divisions of a box or drawer. As it is quite a simple joint it is used for early woodwork exercises.

Before starting to make the joint the wood must be correctly planed to width and thickness. The stages in making the joint are as follows:—

1. Consider carefully the position of the joint. The joint will generally be in the centre of the pieces of wood. Consider also the angle between the two pieces of wood if this is not to be a right angle.
2. Mark on both pieces of wood, the width of the part that is to be cut out. This is best marked with a marking knife (see Section 3). If the joint is to form a right angle the knife will be used against the try-square (see Section 4). The width of the piece that is to be cut out will, of course, be the width of the piece that is to fit into it.

3. Set a marking gauge to half the thickness of the wood. Gauge both pieces using the gauge from the face side in each case.
4. Saw down to the gauge line with a tenon saw (see Section 5). The saw cut must be made in the waste wood or the joint will be loose. The bottom of the upper piece will be cut out, and the top of the lower piece. If the joint is a wide one it is helpful to make several saw cuts down to the gauge line in the waste wood of the joint.
5. Hold the wood in the vice and chisel out the waste wood. Work from both sides so as to meet in the middle. Use the chisel with the bevel uppermost and use as wide a chisel as possible.
6. The joint should, of course, fit straight away. If it is too loose nothing can be done about it. If it is too tight a little wood may be pared away until it fits correctly (see Section 14).

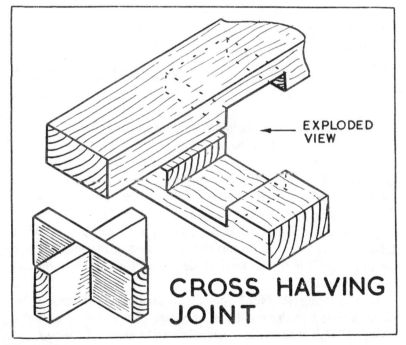

EXPLODED VIEW

CROSS HALVING JOINT

Questions
1. Reproduce the drawing of a cross halving joint.
2. Give two examples of the use of a cross halving joint.

3. Complete the following sentence correctly, using (a) or (b): When using the chisel to pare out the waste wood of a cross halving joint, the bevel of the chisel should be (a) on top, (b) underneath.

4. The saw cuts, made when cutting the joint, are made in the waste wood. Why is this?

SECTION 11

HALVING JOINTS

Halving joints are used mainly for joining together the parts of a framework. They could be used, for example, to join the framework of a small door or cabinet. In addition to the cross halving joint described in Section 10, several other types of halving joint are in general use. These are illustrated opposite.

The halving joint used to join two pieces of wood to form a corner, is called either an angle halving, a corner halving or an L halving (see No. 1 opposite). The method of marking out and cutting is similar to the method described for the cross halving (see Section 10).

The T halving (see No. 2 opposite) is used to join the end of one piece of wood to the middle of another. Sometimes the joint is 'stopped', that is to say it is not taken right across the wood.

If the parts of a frame have to be made in such a way that they cannot pull apart, a dovetail T halving joint is used (see No. 3 opposite). These joints are sometimes sloped on one side only

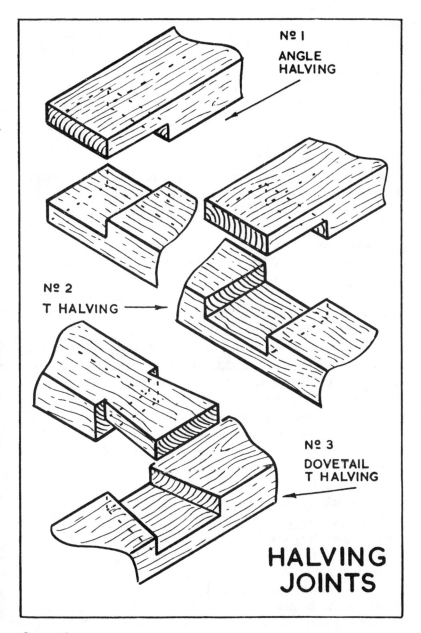

No 1
ANGLE HALVING

No 2
T HALVING

No 3
DOVETAIL
T HALVING

HALVING JOINTS

Questions
1. Name three types of halving joint.
2. Draw two of the halving joints shown above.

[29]

WOOD

Wood is obtained from a tree. The type of wood will depend on the type of tree. Thus beech must come from a beech tree, box from a box tree. Deal, which is the name sometimes given to a softwood in general use, does not come from a deal tree. It comes from one of several types of pine tree.

Wood must be dried before it is fit to use. This drying process is called seasoning.

A tree consists of roots, a trunk, branches and leaves. The function of the roots is to collect plant food from the moisture in the ground. The roots also hold the tree firmly in the ground. The trunk provides wood for the woodworker. On big trees the larger branches may also be used to provide wood. The main function of the branches is to spread out the leaves so that they can collect air and sunlight. These are needed to combine with the plant food to produce growth in the tree.

The drawing shows how a plank of wood is cut out of a tree. The fibres which form the wood may be imagined as strands of string, all of which run up and down the trunk. Thus when the plank is cut out of the tree in the position shown in the drawing, the fibres will run along the plank. These fibres are called the 'grain' of the wood.

When the fibres are cut across, as on the end of the plank shown, the part cut is known as the end grain, because the ends of the fibres are exposed.

When a branch grows out of the trunk, the fibres (the grain) run along the branch but not in line with those in the trunk. Imagine the fibres as string and you will remember better why the result is called a knot in the wood.

A plank is not always cut out of the tree in such a way that the fibres run straight down the plank. This may cause some trouble when you come to plane the wood. You may find you are planing 'against the grain' and the result may be better if the wood is planed in the opposite direction. Wood taken from the branches may have twisting grain which is difficult to plane smoothly from either direction.

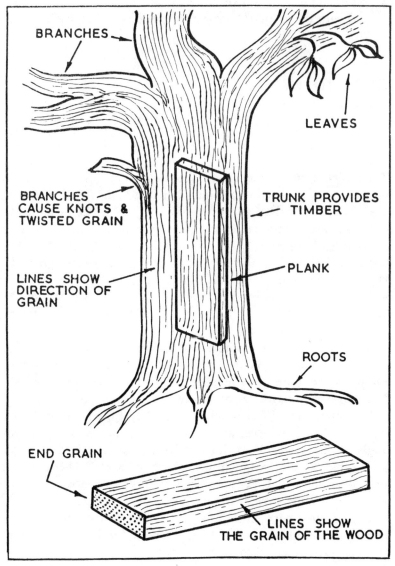

BRANCHES

LEAVES

BRANCHES
CAUSE KNOTS &
TWISTED GRAIN

TRUNK PROVIDES
TIMBER

LINES SHOW
DIRECTION OF
GRAIN

PLANK

ROOTS

END GRAIN

LINES SHOW
THE GRAIN OF THE WOOD

Questions

1 Reproduce the drawing of a plank. Show the grain and the end grain.

2. What is the cause of knots in a plank of wood ?

3. Name four parts of a tree and state one function of each part.

4. Show by means of a sketch what you understand by planing (*a*) with the grain, (*b*) against the grain (see Section 7).

SECTION 13

THE FIRMER CHISEL

The chisel is one of the most important woodworking tools. It is used mainly for cutting joints, but it is also used for cutting out any required shapes in wood and for paring (see Section 14).

Chisels are obtainable in several different sizes, the size being the width of the blade. The smallest size is 3 mm wide. The largest chisel that is normally used in schools is 25 mm wide. However, chisels up to 38 mm wide are obtainable.

The blade of the chisel is made of cast steel (see Section 33 No. 4), hardened and tempered. The blade has a pointed 'tang' which fits into the handle, with a shoulder to prevent it going too far into the handle and splitting it. The best chisel handles are made of boxwood, which is hard and close grained, though some quite good handles are made of red beech or ash. In recent years plastic handles have become popular.

The square edged firmer chisel is in general use for most bench work. When it is necessary to work with the chisel within an angle of less than 90° as, for example, when cutting a dovetail joint, the bevelled edge firmer chisel is used. The drawing opposite shows that a square edge chisel is not satisfactory for working in acute-angled corners.

The bevelled edge chisel is not as strong as the square edged chisel. It should not, therefore, be used for heavy chopping. It is generally reserved for lighter work.

[32]

When using the chisel, great care must be taken to keep the hands, and indeed all parts of the body, behind the cutting edge of the chisel. This warning should not be taken lightly. The writer was acquainted with one man who died with a chisel in his stomach, and another who narrowly escaped death with a chisel in the artery of his wrist.

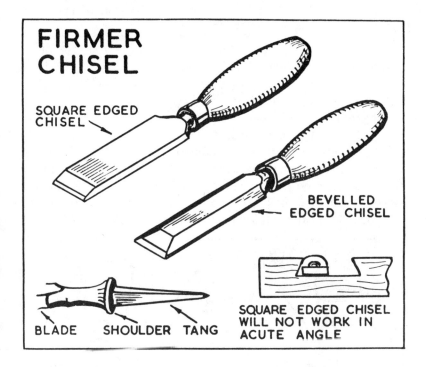

FIRMER CHISEL

SQUARE EDGED CHISEL

BEVELLED EDGED CHISEL

BLADE   SHOULDER   TANG

SQUARE EDGED CHISEL WILL NOT WORK IN ACUTE ANGLE

Questions

1. Reproduce the drawing of one of the chisels shown above.
2. Name an important safety rule that must be followed when using a chisel.
3. Name two types of chisel.
4. Complete the following sentence correctly using (*a*) or (*b*): When cutting within corners of less than 90°, (*a*) a bevelled edge chisel is used, (*b*) a square edged chisel is used.
5. Name (*a*) the material used to make the blade of a chisel, and (*b*) two materials that are used to make handles for chisels.

USING THE CHISEL

The woodwork performed with chisels may be divided into three main groups: chopping, paring, and shaping.

Chopping may be done across the grain of the wood, as when cutting out a mortise (see Section 28). It may also be done along the grain of the wood, as when cutting an angle halving joint (see Section 11). When chopping, the chisel is held in one hand only, the other hand using the mallet. The chisel must be firmly held and positioned with care. It should never be knocked sideways with the mallet, even if it becomes stuck in the wood, as this might break the fairly brittle blade of the chisel. Chopping

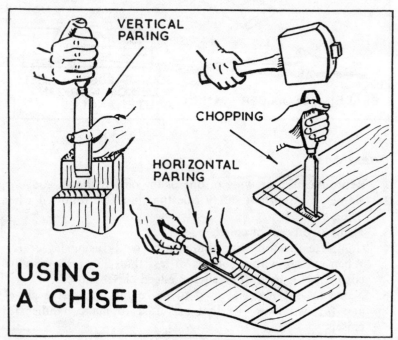

VERTICAL PARING

CHOPPING

HORIZONTAL PARING

USING A CHISEL

along the grain of the wood is only possible if the wood has straight grain. The chisel follows the grain of the wood.

Paring is used for removing comparatively small quantities of wood. When paring, the flat side of the chisel is always next to the wood. The mallet is not used for paring, but the handle of the chisel is sometimes struck with the palm of the hand. The chisel is held in both hands, one holding the blade in order to give complete control over the chisel. The drawing opposite shows typical examples of paring.

Sometimes it is necessary to cut wood out to a certain shape. When this is being done the bevel of the chisel is often used next to the wood. It is then possible to lever on the bevel, either to prevent the chisel cutting too deeply, or to lift the wood out as when cutting the wood from a mortice.

The chisel must always be used with great care, with the hands always behind the cutting edge. A sharp chisel is safer than a blunt one as the sharp chisel requires less pressure to cut.

Questions

1. Make a sketch to show how the chisel is held when chopping.
2. Make a sketch to show one way the chisel may be held when paring.
3. Complete the following sentence correctly, using (*a*) or (*b*): The chisel is held with both hands (*a*) when paring, (*b*) when chopping.
4. Which is safer, a sharp chisel or a blunt one ?

THE MALLET

The mallet is mainly used for striking the wooden handles of chisels when these are being used to make fairly heavy cuts in wood. It is also used for knocking together or apart pieces of wood that are tightly joined. When being used for this latter purpose it is wise to use a piece of waste wood under the mallet to protect the work.

The mallet is nearly always made of red beech. This wood is hard enough to stand up to the heavy work and yet soft enough not to damage the chisel handles.

The handle of the mallet passes right through the head. As the handle is slightly tapered it becomes tighter with use. It

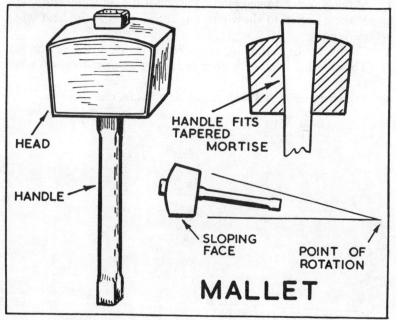

HEAD

HANDLE

HANDLE FITS TAPERED MORTISE

SLOPING FACE

POINT OF ROTATION

MALLET

cannot fly off. It will be seen from the drawing opposite that the striking faces of the mallet slope in slightly towards the bottom. The mallet in use moves through an arc of a circle, the point of rotation being the operator's elbow. The striking faces are sloped in order that they will fall flat on the work (see drawing).

Mallets are made in several weights. The size generally provided for school use weighs about 500 g.

A mallet should never be used to strike metal tools such as nail punches (see Section 18), as this would damage it. Similarly wooden handles of chisels should not be hit with the hammer as this would damage the chisel handle.

Mallets may be quite well made in the school workshop.

Questions

1. Reproduce the drawing of a mallet given opposite.
2. What wood is used to make mallets ?
3. Show by means of a sketch (*a*) how the mallet head is fixed to the handle, (*b*) the reason why the striking faces are sloped inwards towards the handle end.
4. Name two purposes for which a mallet would be used.
5. Complete the following sentence correctly, using (*a*) or (*b*): The mallet is used to strike the handles of chisels (*a*) when a hammer is not available, (*b*) because the mallet does not damage the chisel handle.

SECTION 16

THE HAMMER

The hammer is used mainly for driving nails. It may also be used, for example, for driving in wooden wedges or for striking punches (see Section 18). The hammer should never be used to strike the handles of chisels or screwdrivers.

The type of hammer generally provided for school use is the Warrington pattern cross pein hammer. This has a flat face at one side which is used for most of the work. At the other side is a wedge-shaped cross pein that is used for starting small nails when these are held between the finger and thumb. Some carpenters prefer to have a claw hammer, which has two claws which can be used to pull out nails.

The hammer head is made of drop forged steel, the peins being hardened and tempered. The handle or shaft is generally made of ash or hickory, these are 'elastic' woods which cushion some of the shock from the blow. Metal handles with a rubber hand grip are becoming very popular. This type of handle is almost unbreakable.

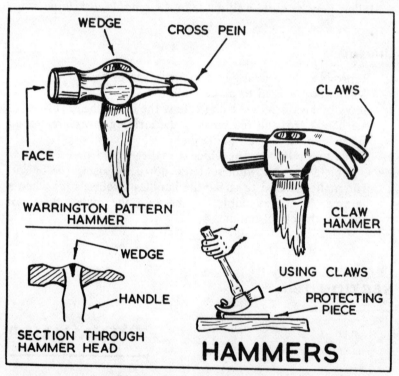

WEDGE   CROSS PEIN

CLAWS

FACE

WARRINGTON PATTERN
HAMMER

CLAW
HAMMER

WEDGE

HANDLE

USING CLAWS

PROTECTING
PIECE

SECTION THROUGH
HAMMER HEAD

HAMMERS

The wooden handle of the hammer is fixed to the head by means of a wedge. The hole through the head is shaped to allow the handle to spread when the wedge is driven in, thus making it almost impossible for the head to fly off (see drawing).

Hammers with loose heads or broken handles should never be used. The head could fly off and might cause a serious injury.

[38]

Hammers are obtainable in several different weights. For small nails a 170 g hammer is suitable; the hammer provided for general purpose bench work in schools generally weighs 340 g; a heavy claw hammer may weigh as much as 680 g.

In use, the hammer should be held near the end of the handle and moved through an arc of a circle in order to bring the face down flat on the nail. Great care should be taken not to damage the surface of wood with the hammer. When removing nails with a claw hammer, a small strip of waste wood should be placed under the head to protect the work.

Questions

1. Reproduce the drawing of one hammer shown opposite.
2. Make a sketch to show how the handle of a hammer is fixed to the head.
3. What material is used to make (a) hammer handles ? (b) hammer heads ?
4. Complete the following sentence correctly, using (a) or (b)· The cross pein of a Warrington pattern hammer is used, (a) for starting small nails, (b) for driving in wedges.
5. Why should a hammer with a loose head not be used ?

SECTION 17

NAILS

Nails are used as a quick and easy method of joining pieces of wood. Nails alone do not make a very strong joint. Several things can be done to make the joint stronger. Glue is often used in conjunction with the nails. In this case the main function of nails is to hold the wood while the glue sets. For outdoor work, where appearance is not of first importance, the nails may be 'clinched' over (see drawing). It is nearly always advisable to 'dovetail' the nails (see drawing). The nails then pull against each other when an attempt is made to separate the two pieces of wood thus joined.

When nailing two pieces of wood of unequal thickness, the nails should be driven through the thin piece into the thick piece.

When using large nails in hardwood, it is often necessary to make a hole first to prevent the wood splitting.

When buying nails three things must be stated: the type of nail; the length of nail; the material or finish of the nail. For example, the nail may be of steel, brass, or galvanized.

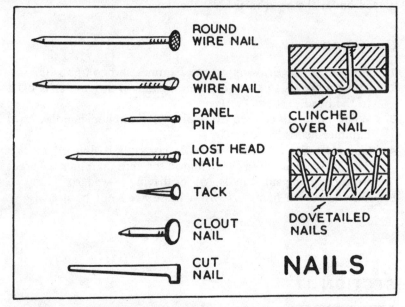

ROUND WIRE NAIL

OVAL WIRE NAIL

PANEL PIN

LOST HEAD NAIL

TACK

CLOUT NAIL

CUT NAIL

CLINCHED OVER NAIL

DOVETAILED NAILS

NAILS

There are a great many different types of nail available. The types of nail in more general use are illustrated above.

Round wire nails—sometimes called French nails—are used for all general purpose work.

Oval wire nails have less tendency to split wood. The small head allows them to be punched below the surface with a nail punch (see Section 18).

Panel pins are obtainable only in small sizes. They are round with very small heads. They are used for light work such as fixing plywood or hardboard.

Lost head nails are larger versions of the panel pin. They are used when the nail is to be punched below the surface of the wood.

Tacks are used mainly for fixing canvas, carpets or upholstery.

Clout nails have large flat heads. They are used, for example, for fixing roofing felt.

Veneer pins are similar to panel pins but very thin.

Cut nails are used mainly by builders, for example, for fixing floorboards.

Questions

1. Describe how you could strengthen a nailed joint (*a*) for outdoor work, (*b*) for indoor work.
2. Reproduce the drawing of nails given on page 40.
3. Show by means of a sketch what is meant by the terms (*a*) dovetailed nails, (*b*) clinched nails.
4. For what purpose would the following nails be used, (*a*) tacks, (*b*) clout nails, (*c*) cut nails, (*d*) French nails ?

SECTION 18

THE NAIL PUNCH

When nails are used, the appearance or efficiency of the finished job is often improved by driving the nails slightly below the surface of the wood. This is done with a nail punch. If, for example, a plywood base is fixed to a box, it is better to punch the nails in, or the nail heads would scratch any surface the box is put on. If also a plywood or hardboard panel is nailed on a door frame, the nails should be punched in. The small cavity thus made may then be filled.

Nail punches are made in several sizes. Always use a nail punch that fits the nail; too large a nail punch would make an unnecessarily large hole. Too small a nail punch would slip off the nail.

Nail punches are made with a hollow point which helps to prevent the punch slipping off the nail. This tends to become flattened and worn on an old punch.

Nail punches are made of cast steel, hardened and tempered at the point.

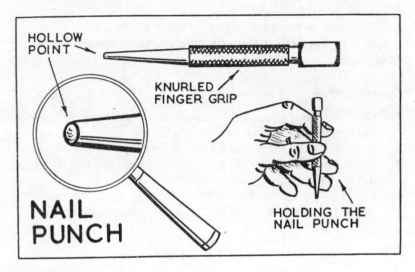

HOLLOW POINT

KNURLED FINGER GRIP

NAIL PUNCH

HOLDING THE NAIL PUNCH

Questions

1. Reproduce the drawing of a nail punch given above.
2. What is a nail punch used for?
3. Why is it advisable to use a nail punch of the correct size?
4. What material is used to make nail punches?

SECTION 19

THE PINCERS

Pincers are used for pulling out nails. If a nail is started at an angle so that there is a danger of its coming out of the side of the wood or splitting the wood then it is better to pull it out with the pincers and start again. If a nail bends over before it is driven right in, it is better pulled out and another used. Many woodworkers rely on secondhand wood for much of their work.

The pincers are used to pull out any nails already in the wood.

The method of using the pincers is important. The nail is gripped as low as possible, and the tool levered sideways (see drawing). In order not to damage the wood, a piece of waste wood or a piece of metal should be placed under the pincers.

A claw is generally made on one leg of the pincers. Although this is not much use for pulling out nails, it is useful for lifting up nails that are bent over.

Pincers are made of drop forged steel.

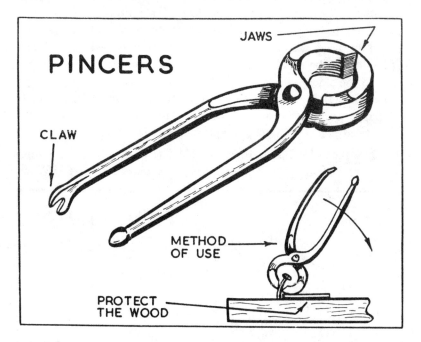

PINCERS

JAWS

CLAW

METHOD OF USE

PROTECT THE WOOD

Questions

1. Reproduce the drawing of a pair of pincers.
2. Make a sketch to show how pincers are used.
3. How would you prevent pincers marking the wood, when pulling a nail out ?

SECTION 20

THE HOUSING JOINT

The housing joint is used mainly for joining shelves to the upright supports. It is also used sometimes for joining divisions and partitions to the main structure. For example, a housing joint could be used when making bookshelves or a bedside cabinet. It could also be used to attach the central division of a small tool tray to the sides.

Before starting to make the joint, the wood must be correctly prepared to width and thickness. The stages in making the joint to attach a shelf to a sidepiece are as follows:—

1. The piece that is to form the shelf (part A on the drawing) must be cut to length and the ends planed square. When

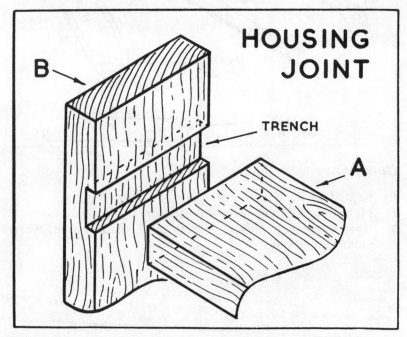

HOUSING JOINT

B

TRENCH

A

cutting to length an allowance must be made for the depth of the joint, usually about 6 mm.

2. The position of the top face of the shelf is marked on the upright (drawing, part B). This is squared across the wood on the inside face using a marking knife.

3. Place the end of the shelf with the top face on the knife line, and mark the thickness of the shelf on the upright piece. Square this mark across with the knife.

4. Square these knife lines round the edges of the upright using a sharp pencil (see No. 1, page 45).

5. Set the gauge to the depth of the housing and gauge between the pencil lines. The gauge is used from the inside face of the wood.

6. Saw down to the gauge line, making each sawcut up to the line but in the waste wood. If the board is a wide one, it may be helpful to make a chisel cut for the saw to run in (see No. 2, page 45).

7. Chisel out the waste wood, working from each side of the board. Level the bottom of the housing by paring lightly (see No. 3, page 45).

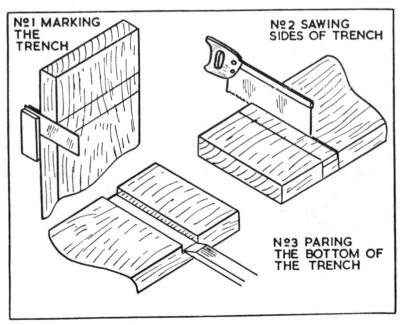

Nº1 MARKING THE TRENCH

Nº2 SAWING SIDES OF TRENCH

Nº3 PARING THE BOTTOM OF THE TRENCH

8. If the marking has been accurately done and the work carefully performed, the joint should fit perfectly first time.

Questions

1. Reproduce the drawing of a through housing joint.
2. Give two examples of the use of a housing joint.
3. When the position of the housing has been marked on the uprights with knife lines, these lines are squared round the edges with a pencil. Why is a pencil used here and not a knife? (revise Section 3).
4. Imagine that you are asked to make a bookshelf using housing joints. The inside measurement between the uprights is 500 mm. How long would you make the shelves?

SECTION 21

THE BRADAWL

The bradawl is used for making small holes in wood before using screws or nails. It is suitable for making holes only for small screws. The bradawl is also frequently used to mark the position of a hole that has to be drilled. For example, when hanging a door, the position of the screws is marked through the hinge with a bradawl. The hinge may then be taken away and the holes drilled.

Bradawls are obtainable in several different sizes. The smaller the size the thinner the blade. The handle of the bradawl is made of beech or ash with a ferrule to prevent it splitting. The blade is made of tool steel.

The end of the bradawl blade is sharpened on both sides to form a chisel point. When making a hole the chisel edge is placed across the grain in order to cut the fibres. The bradawl is pushed a little way into the wood and then given a twist. It is then pushed in a little further and given another twist and so on

The bradawl is also removed from the wood with a twisting action.

The blade of the bradawl can be broken easily. Care should be taken that it is not bent sideways in use. Spare blades are obtainable quite cheaply.

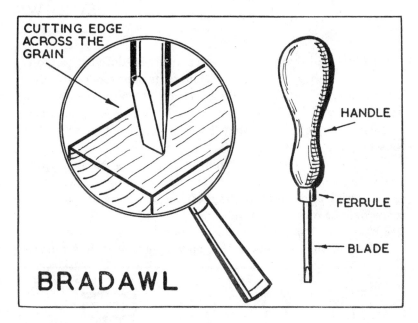

CUTTING EDGE
ACROSS THE
GRAIN

BRADAWL

HANDLE

FERRULE

BLADE

Questions

1. Reproduce the drawing of a bradawl given above.
2. Complete the following sentence correctly, using (*a*) or (*b*): In use, the chisel edge of the bradawl is started into the wood (*a*) across the grain, (*b*) along the grain.
3. Give three examples of the use of a bradawl.

Screws are used by the woodworker for many different purposes. For example, they may be used to join parts of a wooden structure. They may be used to attach fitments such as hinges, door bolts or handles to wood. They are also used sometimes to join parts in such a way that they may be easily removed or shifted by loosening the screws.

When buying screws four things must be stated: the type of screw, the length of screw, the thickness or gauge of screw and the material or surface coating of the screw. For example a screw may be ordered as follows:—

8 gauge × 38 mm steel countersunk.

The gauge or thickness of the screw is indicated by a number.

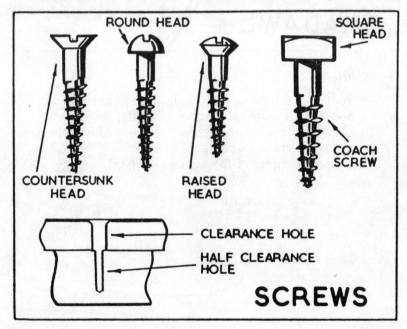

SCREWS

The larger the number, the thicker the screw. Thus a 12g. ×
38 mm is thicker than an 8g. × 38 mm. Some useful sizes are as
follows:— 4g. × 13 mm, 6g. × 19 mm, 8g. × 25 mm, 10g. ×
38 mm, 12g. × 50 mm.

It is necessary to drill holes in the wood to receive all but the
smallest screws. The hole for the shank of the screw should be a
clearance hole, *i.e.* slightly larger than the shank. The hole for
the threaded part should be half the size used for the shank.

When using brass screws in hardwood it is advisable to put in
a steel screw first, since brass screws break off very easily. A
little soap on the thread helps the screw to be driven into the
wood easily.

Screws do not grip very well when used in end grain. For
this reason they are seldom used for this purpose.

The main types of screw head are illustrated opposite. Countersunk head screws are in general use for all woodwork. Round
head screws are used for fixing metal fittings that are not countersunk. Raised head screws combine the advantages of both the
countersunk and round head screws and are neater than both in
appearance. Coach screws are used where a bolt would be more
desirable, but for some reason cannot be used.

Steel countersunk head screws are always in a packet with a
green label. Brass screws have a yellow label and black japanned
screws have a blue label.

When choosing the type and size of screw for a particular job,
common sense must be the main guide. The screw must be
long enough to hold, but not unnecessarily long. If there is any
danger of the wood splitting, thin screws should be used.

Questions
1. Reproduce the drawing of screw heads shown opposite.
2. Complete the following sentence correctly, putting (*a*) or (*b*)
   in the correct place: When drilling holes for a screw, the
   hole for the threaded part should be . . . . the size of
   the hole for the shank. (*a*) twice, (*b*) half.
3. When buying screws four things must be stated. What are
   they ?
4. Arrange the following screws in two columns headed Thick
   and Thin:
(*a*) 2g. × 13 mm, 4g. × 13 mm. (*b*) 8g. × 50 mm, 10g. × 50 mm.
(*c*) 8g. × 32 mm, 4g × 32 mm. (*d*) 6g. × 19 mm, 4g. × 19 mm.

SECTION 23

THE SCREWDRIVER

The screwdriver is used, of course, mainly to turn wood screws (see Section 22). It is also used, for example, when adjusting a mortise gauge (see Section 26) or for taking apart the cutting iron of a plane (see Section 8).

Screwdrivers are obtainable in several different sizes. The size is generally indicated by the length of the blade. The tip of the blade is made smaller and thinner in the shorter sizes. Screwdrivers with 150 mm or 200 mm blades are useful for general work. A 'dumpy' screwdriver with a very small overall length is useful for work in confined spaces.

The pattern of screwdriver generally provided for school workshops is the cabinet pattern (see drawing). The wooden handle is oval in section. It is made of beech or box. The blade has a flat tang which fits through a slotted ferrule on the handle. The blade is thus securely held. Plastic handles have become popular in recent years.

Ratchet screwdrivers have a small ratchet fitted into the handle which allows the handle to be turned without turning the blade. A small button on the handle may be set to grip on the forward stroke only, on the return stroke only, or on both. Ratchet screwdrivers are not suitable for very heavy work.

The tip of the blade must fit the screw that is to be turned. The screw head will be one of two main types. It will have either a straight slotted head (the majority of screws are of this type) or it will have e.g. a Phillips recessed head. Phillips screwdrivers must be used to turn these recessed head screws. Not only must the screwdriver blade be the correct form for the screw, it must also be approximately the correct size. The tip of the blade should be quite a tight fit in the head, it should fit to the bottom of the slot in the screw head. If the screwdriver is too wide it will damage the wood round the screw. If it is too small an excessive strain is placed on the screwdriver tip and the screw head will be damaged.

The tip of the screwdriver should be examined from time to time to see if it has become worn. If worn it may be lightly trimmed on a grindstone, care being taken not to overheat the blade. The blade is made of cast steel hardened and tempered at the tip. If this were allowed to become hot the temper would be removed or drawn.

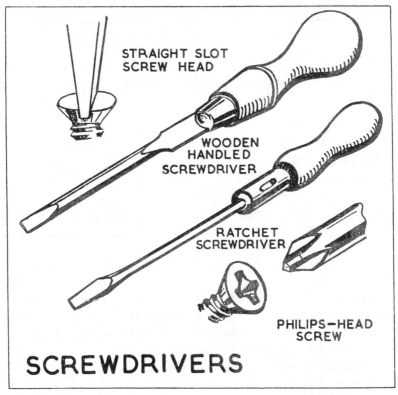

STRAIGHT SLOT SCREW HEAD

WOODEN HANDLED SCREWDRIVER

RATCHET SCREWDRIVER

PHILIPS—HEAD SCREW

SCREWDRIVERS

With regard to care of the screwdriver, three points should be borne in mind. The screwdriver should not be used as a lever, which might bend the blade and it would not then turn true. The handle should never be struck with a hammer, which would roughen the handle making it uncomfortable to hold. The rule followed when using a chisel, namely, that the hands are kept behind the cutting edge, applies also to the screwdriver.

It must be said in favour of the recessed head screw that the screwdriver cannot slip out of the screw and in recent years screws of this type have been sold as Posidriv screws.

Questions

1. Reproduce the drawing of a cabinet pattern screwdriver.
2. Reproduce the drawing showing the tip of a Phillips screwdriver and recessed head screw.
3. State three things that should be borne in mind with regard to the care of the screwdriver.
4. Give one reason (*a*) why a wide screwdriver is not used to turn a small screw, and (*b*) why a small screwdriver is not used to turn a large screw.
5. Name (*a*) the material used to make screwdriver blades, and (*b*) two materials used to make screwdriver handles.

SECTION 24

THE G CRAMP

The G cramp is so called because when viewed from the side it forms the letter G.

Often when it is required to hold two or more pieces of wood together for gluing, drilling or screwing, the G cramp is used. When a piece of wood is being worked on the bench top, the G cramp is often used to hold it firmly in position. When parts of a structure are being assembled, the G cramp is sometimes used to hold them in position.

G cramps are made in several different sizes. The size is the distance between the jaws when fully open. 100 mm, 150 mm and 200 mm cramps are usually provided for school workshops.

The shoe on the end of the screw thread (see drawing) is made to swivel in order that it will always lie flat even when the surfaces being cramped are not parallel. In order to prevent damage to the wood surface, it is always advisable to use waste wood under the jaws of the cramp. A drop of oil on the screw thread and on the swivel shoe helps to keep these moving freely.

The main body of the cramp is made either of malleable cast iron or drop forged steel and the screw is of mild steel.

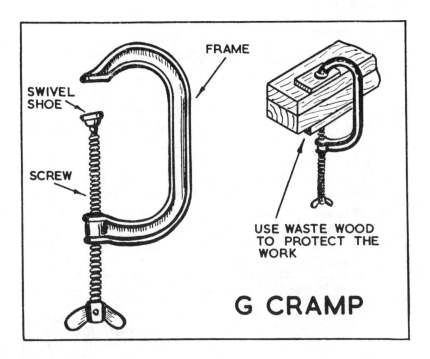

FRAME

SWIVEL SHOE

SCREW

USE WASTE WOOD TO PROTECT THE WORK

G CRAMP

Questions

1. Reproduce the drawing of a G cramp shown above.
2. Give three examples of the use of a G cramp.
3. How would you protect the surface of the wood being cramped in order that it is not marked ?

THE MORTISE AND TENON JOINT

The mortise and tenon joint is used more frequently than any other joint in woodwork. It is used, for example, to join the rails to the legs of a table chair or stool. It is used to join parts of a strong framework such as a door or window frame. It is a very strong joint. There are very many types of mortise and tenon joint, each of which is designed to fulfil special requirements.

The mortise is the name given to the square hole which forms one part of the joint. The tenon is the name given to the part which is cut out to fit into the mortise. The joint relies for much of its strength on the tight fitting of the shoulders.

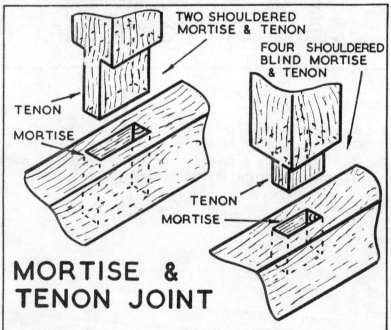

MORTISE & TENON JOINT

The tenon is generally made $\frac{1}{3}$ the thickness of the wood being used. This is not a hard and fast rule. The thickness of the mortise is partly controlled by the width of chisel available.

Several identical joints often have to be made on the same structure. When this is so, they would normally all be marked out at the same time to avoid the re-setting of tools.

When chopping out the mortise there is a tendency for the wood to split, particularly if the joint is near the end. This may be prevented by tightening a G cramp on the wood round the joint. When joints are to be chopped in several pieces of wood they may all be cramped together in this way. When chopping a mortise the wood should be fixed on top of the bench and held either with a holdfast (see Section 33, No. 2) or a G cramp (see Section 24). The wood tends to slip if held in the vice.

The drawing on the left opposite shows a simple two-shouldered mortise and tenon joint. The tenon is made to go right through the wood. The drawing on the right shows a four-shouldered mortise and tenon joint that is 'blind', that is to say, it does not go right through.

Questions

1. Reproduce the drawing of one mortise and tenon joint shown opposite.
2. Name three examples of the use of a mortise and tenon joint.
3. Complete the following sentence correctly, using (a) or (b): A blind mortise is one which (a) passes right through the wood, (b) does not pass right through the wood.
4. State the normal thickness of the tenon in relation to the thickness of the wood used.
5. Name one safety precaution that is taken to prevent the wood splitting when cutting a mortise?

SECTION 26

THE MORTISE GAUGE

The main difference between the mortise gauge and the marking gauge (see Section 9) is that the mortise gauge has two spurs. It may therefore be used to mark two parallel lines at the same time. This is required particularly when marking mortise and tenon joints (see Section 25), but it is also useful on other occasions. For example, it may be used to mark tongues and grooves.

Before attempting to set the mortise gauge, the set screw must be released. When the set screw is unscrewed, the stock is free to slide on the stem and the thumbscrew may be turned to adjust the moveable spur.

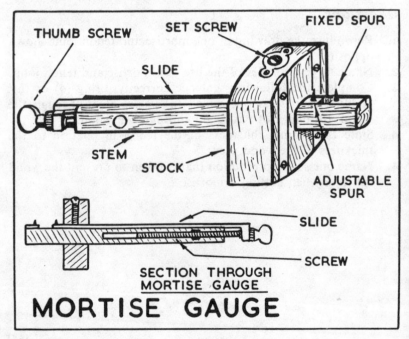

MORTISE GAUGE

When setting the mortise gauge, two settings are necessary. First the distance between the spurs is set; this will be the thickness of the tenon. The end spur is fixed, and the spur nearest the stock is adjusted by turning the thumbscrew. The second setting is the distance between the adjustable spur and the stock; this will be the space allowed between the edge of the mortise and the face side of the wood.

When the gauge is set, the set screw is tightened and the setting is checked.

The method of using the mortise gauge is the same as for the marking gauge. The stroke is made away from the operator. The stock is pressed firmly on the face edge of the wood and the spurs are trailed.

The wooden parts of the mortise gauge are traditionally made of rosewood. This is hard and close grained. The metal parts are brass, with the exception of the spurs which are tool steel.

Questions

1. Reproduce the drawing of a mortise gauge given opposite.
2. The mortise gauge requires two settings. Describe these.
3. Complete the following sentence correctly, using (a) or (b): Before attempting to set the mortise gauge (a) the spurs must be adjusted, (b) the set screw must be released.
4. State three things you know about the method of using a mortise gauge.
5. What wood is used to make mortise gauges ?

THE MORTISE CHISEL

The mortise chisel is used only for chopping out mortises. The heavy work involved when chopping out a large mortise imposes great strain on the chisel. The mortise chisel is therefore made very strongly.

For very heavy work such as chopping out the mortise for an oak gate, a heavy duty mortise chisel would be used. The blade of this is very thick; it is fitted with a large sturdy handle. Heavy duty mortise chisels are not much used in school workshops.

The socket mortise chisel is a very efficient tool. Normally chisel blades have a tang which fits into the handle, the handle

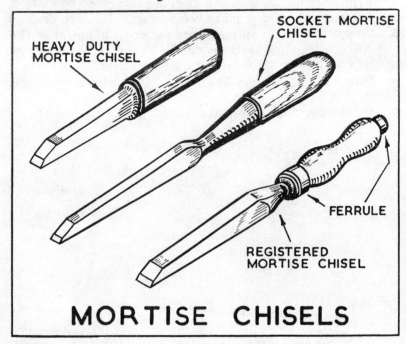

HEAVY DUTY MORTISE CHISEL

SOCKET MORTISE CHISEL

FERRULE

REGISTERED MORTISE CHISEL

MORTISE CHISELS

being fitted with a ferrule to stop it splitting. In the case of the socket chisel, the handle fits into a socket that is formed on the blade to receive it, which helps to prevent the handle splitting even with continual hard work.

The registered pattern chisel does not have such a thick blade as the two chisels mentioned above. The heavy duty and socket chisels are seldom obtained in widths of more than 13 mm, but the registered chisel is obtainable in widths up to 25 mm. The chief characteristic of the registered chisel is the steel ferrule on top of the handle. The great disadvantage of this is that it spoils the working face of the mallet.

A leather washer is placed between the blade and handle of mortise chisels. This helps to cushion the shock of heavy mallet blows.

The blade of the chisel is made of hardened and tempered cast steel. The handle is generally made of boxwood or plastic but red beech is occasionally used.

Questions

1. Name three types of mortise chisel.
2. Reproduce the drawing of one mortise chisel shown opposite.
3. For what purpose is a mortise chisel used?
4. Complete the following sentence correctly, using (a) or (b): A disadvantage of the registered pattern chisel is (a) that it tends to damage the mallet, (b) that it is hardened and tempered.
5. Mortise chisels are fitted with a leather washer. Where is this fitted and why ?

MAKING A MORTISE AND

TENON JOINT

The stages in making a simple two-shouldered mortise and tenon joint are shown in the sketches opposite.

The wood must be accurately prepared to width and thickness before making the joint.

1. Mark the shoulders of the tenon (piece A on the drawing). As the tenon in this joint is to pass right through the wood the length of the tenon will be the same as the depth of the piece of wood in which the mortise is made. It is usual to add about 1-2 mm to the length of the tenon in order to allow a little to smooth off when the joint is finished.

2. Mark the position of the mortise (part B on the drawing). Square these marks round one side and two edges of the wood with a sharp pencil.

3. Set the mortise gauge (see Section 26). The distance between the spurs should be approximately $\frac{1}{3}$ the thickness of the wood. The spurs must be set to bring the mortise in the centre of the wood.

4. Use the gauge from the face side of both pieces of wood. Mark between the pencil lines of the mortise and right round the end of the tenon.

5. Cut the cheeks of the tenon using a tenon saw (see drawing). Take care to follow the gauge lines.

6. Cut the shoulders of the tenon. Use the tenon saw with the wood on the bench hook. Take care to saw in the waste wood beside the line.

7. Drill a series of holes to remove most of the waste wood from the mortise (some craftsmen prefer to drill only one

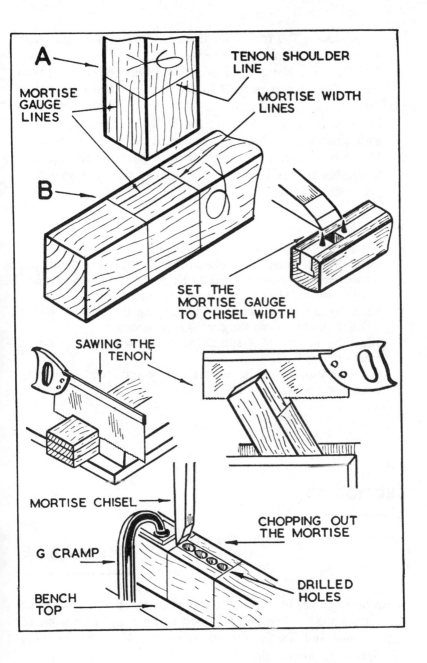

A

TENON SHOULDER LINE

MORTISE GAUGE LINES

MORTISE WIDTH LINES

B

SET THE MORTISE GAUGE TO CHISEL WIDTH

SAWING THE TENON

MORTISE CHISEL

CHOPPING OUT THE MORTISE

G CRAMP

DRILLED HOLES

BENCH TOP

hole). Use a brace fitted with a bit slightly smaller than the thickness of the mortise. Drill from either side to meet in the middle. The reason for these holes is to allow the waste to break away better when being cut .

8. Chop out the waste wood of the mortise. Work from both sides of the wood to meet in the middle. Keep the flat of the chisel towards the ends of the mortise all the time. Do not lever with the chisel on the ends of the mortise. The ends must be kept sharp and square.

9. It is not considered good practice to pare the sides of the tenon, but the inside faces of the mortise can be cleared until a smooth fit is obtained.

Questions

1. A tenon is to pass through the mortise made in a piece of wood 38 mm square. What length would the tenon be made?

2. A mortise and tenon joint is to be made in a piece of wood 25 mm square. How thick would the tenon be made?

3. Show by means of sketches, (*a*) cutting the shoulders of a tenon, and (*b*) cutting the cheeks of a tenon.

4. Show by means of a sketch how you would chop out a mortise.

5. For what purpose might you use a brace and bit when making a mortise and tenon joint.

SECTION 29

THE BRACE

When boring holes in wood of more than 6 mm diameter, a brace and bit are used. The brace is used to hold and turn a bit of suitable type and size for the job in hand. A number of types and sizes of bit are obtainable.

Braces are of two main types: plain and ratchet. The ratchet brace has a strong ratchet built into the frame. This may be set to allow the bit to remain stationary either on the forward or return stroke as the brace is rotated. The ratchet is very useful when working in confined spaces that do not allow a full sweep of the brace. Most school workshops have at least one ratchet brace.

The size of the brace is indicated by the length of the sweep. The sweep is the diameter of the circle formed when turning the crank of the brace (see drawing). The sweep may vary from 125 mm to 300 mm. The brace provided for school use usually has a 200 mm sweep.

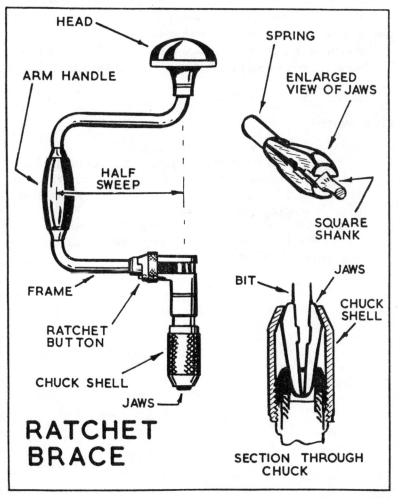

HEAD

ARM HANDLE

SPRING

ENLARGED VIEW OF JAWS

HALF SWEEP

SQUARE SHANK

FRAME

RATCHET BUTTON

CHUCK SHELL

JAWS

RATCHET BRACE

BIT

JAWS

CHUCK SHELL

SECTION THROUGH CHUCK

The bits are held in the brace in a two-jaw chuck. When the chuck shell is screwed up, the two jaws are tightened firmly on to the square taper shank of the bit. On most braces the jaws are designed to hold only square taper shank bits and not parallel shank drills. When fitting bits into the chuck it is important to make sure that the whole of the square taper shank is correctly fitted into the jaws (see drawing).

The jaws are held together by a small spring clip. They fit into a slot in the chuck which allows them to open and close but prevents them turning round.

When using the brace and bits, great care must be taken to ensure that holes are not bored in the bench. Great care should also be taken of the delicate cutting edges of the bits.

The metal parts of the brace are made of steel. The wooden handles are made of some suitable hardwood such as beech or of plastic material.

Questions

1. Reproduce the drawing of a ratchet brace.
2. Make a sketch to show how the jaws of a brace hold a bit.
3. Complete the following sentence correctly, using (a) or (b):
   The jaws of a brace are designed to hold (a) parallel shank drills, (b) square taper shank bits.
4. What do you understand by the "sweep" of a brace?
5. The ratchet brace has one important advantage over the plain brace. What is this?

SECTION 30

THE TWIST BIT

The type of bit that is probably used more than any other, when boring holes in wood, is the twist bit, sometimes called an auger bit. There are several types of twist bit. The most common type, which is also the one generally provided for school use, is the Jennings pattern twist bit. The details of this are shown in the drawing on page 66.

When using the twist bit to bore a hole, the centre of the hole should first be carefully marked. The point of the screw is accurately placed on this before starting to bore. If the hole is to be bored right through the wood, it is usual to work from both sides in order to prevent the wood splitting out at the back. The hole is bored through the wood until the screwed end of the bit appears on the other side. The wood is then turned round, the screwed end placed in the small centre hole, and the boring completed.

The majority of holes have to be bored square with the wood. The accuracy of the boring may be tested by placing the try-square on the wood. The blade of the square is then 'sighted' with the bit to see if the two are parallel.

It may be necessary to bore holes to a certain depth. This may be done using an adjustable depth stop attachment. Many workshops have one of these (see drawing). The stop is set to allow the required amount of bit to enter the wood. Simple depth stops may be made by boring a hole through a small piece of wood and slipping this onto the bit, so that only the required amount of bit is able to enter the work (see drawing).

Great care must be taken with the bits. Small diameter bits become bent easily and are thus spoiled. The screw, spurs, and cutters of a twist bit are very easily damaged if dropped or knocked on metal tools. Bits *can* be sharpened, however, but this should be rarely necessary.

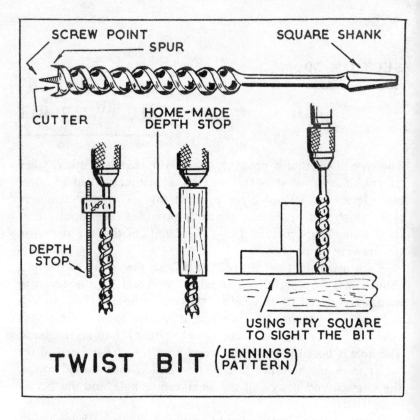

SCREW POINT
SPUR
SQUARE SHANK
CUTTER
HOME-MADE
DEPTH STOP
DEPTH
STOP
USING TRY SQUARE
TO SIGHT THE BIT

TWIST BIT (JENNINGS PATTERN)

Questions

1. Reproduce the drawing of a twist bit.
2. Name (*a*) the type of twist bit generally used in schools, (*b*) an alternative name for the twist bit.
3. When drilling a hole right through a piece of wood using a twist bit, the wood may split out at the back. How would you prevent this ?
4. Make a sketch to show (*a*) a depth stop attachment that may be used on a twist bit, (*b*) a simple depth stop device that you could make.

THE COUNTERSINK BIT

When screws are being used, a hole is drilled to take the screw (see Section 22). When countersunk head screws are being used, it is usual to make a small recess called a countersink at the mouth of the hole. This allows the head of the screw to sink just below the level of the surrounding wood. A neat and strong job is thus made.

Countersink bits are of two main types: rosehead bits and snailshorn bits. The main parts of these are shown below. The rosehead bit has a series of cutters, nine in all, that radiate from the centre point. These cutters do not look much like the petals of a rose, but the similarity is sufficient to give the bit its name. The snailshorn bit has two cutting edges which curve away from the point. The curve making it look a little like a snail's shell. The snailshorn bit, with its two cutters, cuts very much more quickly than the rosehead bit with its many cutters.

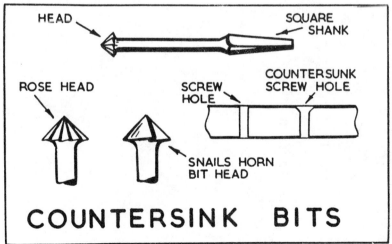

COUNTERSINK BITS

The rosehead bit may also be used for countersinking soft metals such as brass (see Section 33, No. 3).

The point angle of the countersink is 90°, this being the countersink angle of a screw head. The bit has a square taper shank to fit the two jaws of the brace.

Countersink bits are obtainable in several sizes. The size generally provided for school use is 13 mm maximum diameter. This may be used for all the screws in general use.

Questions

1. Reproduce the drawing of a rosehead countersink bit.
2. For what purpose is a countersink bit used?
3. Name two types of countersink bit.
4. Complete the following sentence correctly, using (a) or (b): The point angle of the countersink is 90° (a) because this cuts more quickly, (b) because this is the countersink angle of a wood screw.

BITS IN LESS COMMON USE

The woodworker's brace is used to hold a number of types and sizes of bit. All of these have a square tapered shank which fits in the two jaws of the brace. The two types in most frequent use are the twist bit, sometimes called an auger bit, and the countersink bit (see Sections 30 and 31). In addition to these there are several other types of bit that are used less frequently.

The Shell Bit. This is used for boring holes for screws or small dowels and so on. It is half round in shape and sharpened on the outside to form a cutting edge. It is rather slow cutting,

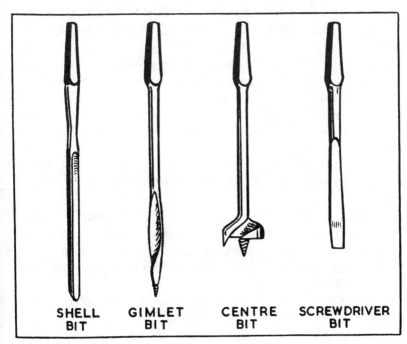

| SHELL | GIMLET | CENTRE | SCREWDRIVER |
| BIT | BIT | BIT | BIT |

but it forms a nice clean hole particularly when cutting into end grain. Shell bits are obtainable only in small sizes.

Some shell bits have a small lip on the cutting edge to pull out the waste from the hole. This is very useful when boring a deep, blind hole.

The Gimlet Bit. This is also used for boring small holes for screws and so forth. It has a screw thread at the point which draws the bit into the wood, and this makes the work somewhat easier. But, as will be seen from the drawing, it has a tapered point and this tends to split the wood.

Centre Bits. There are two types of centre bit. The older type has a plain point. The more modern type has a screw point, and has a rather better cutting action.

Centre bits are quite easily sharpened and this is an advantage, but they have the rather serious disadvantage that they tend to wander sideways when used for boring deep holes. This is because there is hardly any body of the drill behind the cutting edge to keep it in alignment.

When boring right through with a centre bit, the bit is taken through until the point appears. The hole is then finished from the reverse side, otherwise the hole will break out and split the wood.

The Screwdriver Bit. This has a tip exactly the same as a screwdriver. When a large number of screws have to be put in, it is sometimes quicker to use a screwdriver bit in the brace rather than a screwdriver. The brace provides a considerable leverage on the bit. This makes it suitable for removing screws that are very tight.

Screwdriver bits can be made quite well from old twist or centre bits, which can be cut down and drawn out to form a screwdriver tip.

The Forstner Bit. The main feature of the forstner bit is that the centre spur is extremely small leaving the bottom of the hole unmarked. It is used mainly for boring shallow holes and particularly for decorative work where a hole is required with the centre unmarked.

The Expansion Bit. This may be adjusted to cut different sized holes. This is useful particularly in the larger sizes, as it saves the need of having a selection of large drills. The range of the drill is limited. Thus a small one may have a range of say 25 mm to 45 mm, and a large one may have a range of 35 mm to 75 mm.

The size of the hole that can be bored is really limited by the strength of the operator. Even with a brace of 250 mm sweep it is hard work to drill a hole of 75 mm diameter, even in softwood.

The Dowel Trimmer. This is used to take off the corners of the ends of a piece of dowel rod that is being used to make a dowel joint. The bit is obtainable in one size which is suitable for the diameters of dowel rod used for dowel joints.

The Extension Bit. This is used for boring holes in places that would be otherwise inaccessible. It consists of a two-jaw chuck, exactly the same as the two-jaw chuck of the brace. This is fixed to the end of an extension bar. The bar has a square taper shank which fits the jaws of the brace. The required bit is

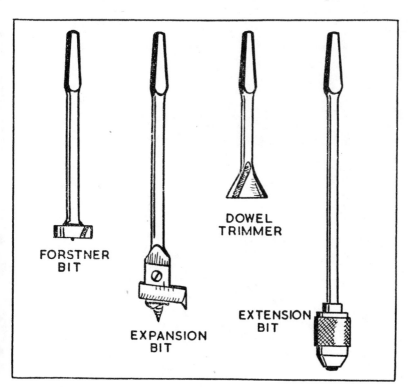

FORSTNER BIT

EXPANSION BIT

DOWEL TRIMMER

EXTENSION BIT

fitted into the chuck on the end of the extension bar and the brace is thus given a much longer reach.

Questions

1. Reproduce the drawing of any two of the bits shown on pages 69 and 71.
2. Complete the following sentence correctly, using (a) or (b): The chief feature of the hole drilled by a Forstner bit is (a) that the bottom of the hole is flat and unmarked, (b) that the hole may be drilled in an inaccessible place.
3. Give one disadvantage of (a) a gimlet bit, (b) a centre bit.
4. Give one example of the use of (a) a shell bit, (b) a screwdriver bit.

SOME USEFUL DEFINITIONS

1. **Bench Hook:** This is sometimes called a sawing board. It is used to support small pieces of wood on the bench that are being sawed with the tenon saw.

2. **Bench Holdfast:** This is a device that is used to hold a piece of wood securely on top of the bench. A hole must be drilled in the top of the bench to take the holdfast. It is not very much used in school workshops. The G cramp is more often used to hold wood on the bench top.

3. **Brass:** A yellow metal used to make parts of tools, screws etc. It does not rust.

4. **Cast Steel:** Sometimes called tool steel or high carbon steel. This type of steel is used for making many tools and tool parts. The most important characteristic of this material is that it can be hardened and tempered. It is then possible to produce a good cutting edge on it as, for example, on chisels or plane irons. It is also possible to produce a hard tough point as on nail punches and screwdrivers.

5. **Ferrule:** A metal ring is usually fitted to wooden handles. The purpose of this is to prevent the handle splitting. The ring is called a ferrule.

6. **Galvanized:** Steel nails and other steel objects are sometimes coated with zinc to prevent them rusting. This process is known as galvanizing.

7. **Kerf:** This is the name given to the amount of wood taken out by a saw cut. The teeth of a saw are set alternately from side to side. This makes the saw kerf wider than the saw. The saw should not then stick or rub in the kerf. A large toothed saw heavily set will make a much wider kerf than a small toothed saw.

8. **Straight Edge:** A straight edge is used to test the straightness of a piece of wood. For much of the small work a 300 mm steel rule makes a good straight edge. Most school work-

shops have a metre steel straight edge.   Larger straight edges are carefully prepared from reliable wood.

9. **Screw Cup:** This is shaped metal washer which is used under the head of a countersunk screw.   Screw cups are used when there is a considerable strain on a screw and a danger of the head digging into the wood.

10. **t.p.i.:** This abbreviation means teeth per inch and it is used to indicate the size of saw teeth. 1 inch is 25·4 mm in length.

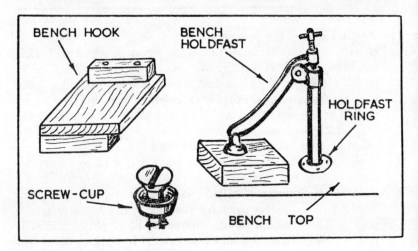

Questions

1. Name three tools that have blades made of cast steel.   (See Sections 8, 13 and 23).

2. Name two tools that have handles fitted with ferrules.   (See Sections 13, and 23).

3. For what purpose would you use (a) a straight edge, (b) a bench hook ?   (See Sections 7 and 1).

4. Describe briefly what is meant by the following terms, (a) kerf, (b) tang   (see Section 13), (c) galvanized.

5. Make a sketch of a bench hook.

REVISION

1. State briefly the purpose for which you would use the following: (*a*) a bench hook, (*b*) a bradawl. (See Sections 33 and 21.)

2. Show, by means of a sketch, the grinding and sharpening angles of a plane blade. (See Section 8.)

3. What types of wood are used to make (*a*) woodwork benches, (*b*) chisel handles, (*c*) hammer handles ? (See Sections 1, 13 and 16.)

4. Name three types of chisel. Give one use for each. (See Sections 13 and 27.)

5. (*a*) Make a sketch to show a tape rule. (*b*) State the number of millimetres in one metre.

6. Make sketches to show (*a*) a Phillips recessed head screw, (*b*) a round wire nail, (*c*) a tack. (See Sections 22 and 17.)

7. Describe how you could test a try-square to see if it is true. (See Section 4.)

8. What does abbreviation T.P.I. stand for ? (See Section 5.)

9. Show by means of a sketch how you would hold a tenon saw. (See Section 5.)

10. A jack plane iron consists of a blade and a cap iron. (*a*) What is the purpose of the cap iron ? (*b*) What happens if the cap iron does not fit well on to the blade ? (See Section 8.)

11. A very important safety rule applies when using chisels. What is this ? (See Section 14.)

12. Name three types of halving joint and draw one of them. (See Sections 10 and 11.)

13. The marking gauge is not a very easy tool to use. Name three things that you should remember when using one. (See Section 9.)

14. State briefly what you understand by the following terms : (*a*) Paring, (*b*) Spur, (*c*) End grain, (*d*) Ferrule, (*e*) Kerf. (See Sections 14, 9, 12 and 33.)

15. When buying nails you would need to state three things. What are they ? (See Section 17.)

16. Describe briefly how you would bore a hole right through a piece of wood, using a brace and twist bit. (See Section 30.)

17. Give one example of the use of (*a*) a housing joint, (*b*) a mortise and tenon joint, and (*c*) a halving joint. (See Sections 20, 10, 11 and 25.)

18. When buying screws, four things must be stated. What are they ? (See Section 22.)

19. Show by means of a sketch (*a*) how the head of a mallet is held on the handle, (*b*) how the head of a hammer is held on the handle, and (*c*) how the blade of a firmer chisel is held in the handle. (See Sections 15, 16 and 13.)

20. What is the difference between an 8 gauge × 38 mm screw and a 10 gauge × 38 mm screw? (See Section 22.)

21. State briefly the purpose for which you would use (*a*) a nail punch, (*b*) a G cramp. (See Sections 18 and 24.)

22. Show by means of sketches what you understand by the following terms: (*a*) a screw cup, (*b*) extension bit. (See Sections 33 and 32.)

23. Make sketches to show (*a*) a hole drilled to take a screw, and (*b*) the hole formed by a countersink bit. (See Sections 22 and 31.)

24. What do you understand by the following terms ? (*a*) The sweep of a brace. (*b*) The cap iron. (*c*) The grinding and sharpening angles. (See Sections 29 and 8.)